BIG RIGS · FIRE TRUCKS
DIGGERS · FARM EQUIPMENT

SEE HOW THEY WORK &
LOOK INSIDE
BIG RIGS

Have you ever thought about how materials for construction get to the sites? They are carried long distances by large trucks called "tractor- trailers." There are trucks for all sorts of other jobs that you may not think about. Some trucks mix concrete, carry logs, dig holes, race each other at high speeds, do stunts, and even swim rivers. Trucks are pretty amazing!

© 2015 Flowerpot Press

Contents under license from Aladdin Books Ltd.

Flowerpot Press
142 2nd Avenue North
Franklin, TN 37064

Flowerpot Press is a Division of Kamalu LLC, Franklin, TN, U.S.A.
and Flowerpot Children's Press Inc., Oakville, ON, Canada.

ISBN: 978-1-4867-0804-8

Editor: Jon Richards

Design: David West Children's Book Design

Designer: Robert Perry

Illustrators: Simon Tegg & Graham White

American Edition Editors: Johannah Gilman Paiva
and Ashley Rideout

American Redesign: Stephanie Meyers

Consultant: John Paiva

Printed in China.

TABLE OF CONTENTS

TRACTORS

The front part of the tractor-trailer truck is called a "tractor." The driver sits inside the cab at the front of the tractor. From here, the driver can steer the trucks along the road. Some cabs may even have beds in the back where drivers can sleep (see pages 16-17)! Beneath the cab is the engine. The engine needs to be very powerful to drive the tractor and pull its load. This engine is as strong as the engines of ten small cars!

BOBTAILING

When a tractor-trailer drives without its trailer (above) it is called "bobtailing."

Fifth wheel skid plate

Behind the cab is a device called the "fifth wheel skid plate" that connects the tractor to a trailer. This special link lets the truck bend in the middle, allowing the truck to turn very tight corners.

Axle seal

The axle seal keeps oil in the gears that turn the wheel to help it move smoothly. It also keeps dirt and debris out of the gear.

Fuel tank

The fuel tank holds the fuel for the tractor's engine. It can hold up to 300 gallons (1,136 liters)!

Shock absorber

Trucks need shock absorbers to prevent any bumps or holes in the road from causing damage to the truck.

Wheels

A tractor has two (or more!) sets of wheels. The front set steers the tractor. The rear sets push the tractor along and carry the weight of the trailer.

Exhaust
[F]umes are created by the engine [a]s it converts fuel into energy. [T]hey are then carried out of the [tr]uck by the exhaust pipe.

Horn
A loud horn warns other drivers of any danger.

Radiator grill
This is where cool air can enter the truck to help keep all the hard-working parts from overheating.

Engine
When the engine has trouble, the whole cab is then tilted forward to let the mechanic reach the engine to fix it.

Early trucks used steam engines instead of diesel engines. In steam powered trucks, water was heated in a boiler to make steam that gave the power to operate the truck.

ALL SHAPES AND SIZES

Trucks come in all shapes and sizes. Steam-powered trucks were smaller than today's trucks since steam isn't as powerful as the fuel we use today. Modern engines allow trucks to be much larger and carry more cargo.

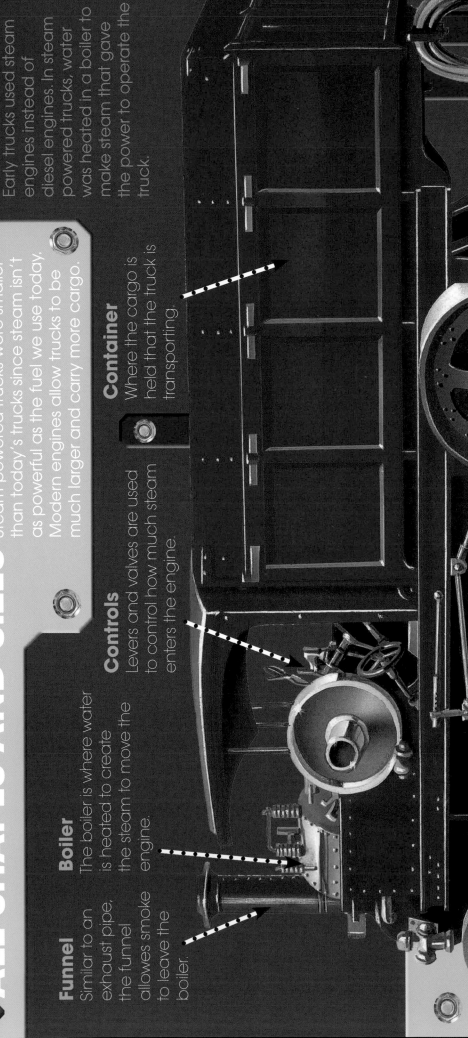

Funnel
Similar to an exhaust pipe, the funnel allowes smoke to leave the boiler.

Boiler
The boiler is where water is heated to create the steam to move the engine.

Controls
Levers and valves are used to control how much steam enters the engine.

Container
Where the cargo is held that the truck is transporting.

Linkage
The steam created in the boiler pushes the linkage bar, causing the wheel to move.

Brake
The brake is also powered by steam from the boiler.

PICKUP TRUCK

One of the most popular types of truck is the pickup truck (above). Behind the cab is a flat bed where the load is carried.

TRACTOR-TRAILER TRUCK

Some trucks have trailers that are pulled by a tractor (below). Between the tractor and the trailer is a special device that allows the truck to bend. Sometimes, a tractor may pull more than one trailer. The longest truck in the world was an Australian road train. Pulling five trailers, this truck was as long as 15 cars, weighed as much as 150 cars, and had 110 wheels!

ONE-PIECE TRUCK

Some trucks come in one piece (above). At the front of the truck is the cab where the driver sits. Behind this, the truck is fitted with a "body unit." This could be a trash compactor, a crane, or a container.

TATE & LYLE
Sugar Refiners

TANKER

Tankers pull special types of trailers. These trailers are designed to carry liquids, such as gasoline or milk. Some tankers have dividers that allow them to carry two or more different types of liquid at the same time without them mixing.

Sleeper
This is where a bunk is sometimes located for a driver to grab a quick nap at a rest stop.

Exhaust pipe

Horn

Radiator
The radiator is found at the front of the engine. Its job is to prevent the engine from overheating by circulating a liquid called "coolant" that cools off the hot engine.

Cabin
The driver sits in a cab that is tiny compared to the rest of the truck.

Headlight
Front lights help drivers see where they are going at night.

Air filter
The tanker's air filter cleans dust and dirt from the air before it goes into the engine.

Fuel tank
Although this truck is carrying fuel, it needs its own fuel as well to provide energy to the engine.

A fuel tanker is filled with either gasoline or diesel at the storage depot. The tanker then carries its load to gas stations. Here, the fuel is pumped out of the tanker and into storage tanks. These storage tanks are usually kept underground.

Ladder

This ladder allows access to the top of the tank so the driver can make sure the liquid is entering the tank correctly.

Liquid in

Liquid is put into the tanker through hatches on the top of the trailer.

Double skin

The trailer is made from two layers of tough metal. These prevent it from splitting open if there is an accident.

Tank trailer

The liquid being transported is stored in this large tank.

Liquid out

Liquid comes out of the tanker through pipes under the trailer.

Drum brake

This special brake is designed to be able to stop a heavy truck traveling at high speeds.

TRAILERS

Trailers are used to carry heavy loads, from trees, to construction equipment, to cars. When it comes to moving cargo long distances, one of the best transportation tools is the trailer. Some trailers are big boxes made for holding smaller things like crates, while others are open and made for hauling large loads.

Heavy load

This large construction truck is an example of a heavy load that needs to be carried by a low trailer.

Lowboy

A trailer that is two different heights, allowing tall equipment to be transported on the lower section.

LOGGING TRUCK

Some trucks carry logs (below). Here, sets of wheels are fixed to either end of the logs. The logs, supports, and wheels together act as a trailer.

Sometimes tractor-trailers are fitted with a low, open trailer. Bigger cargo may need a low trailer so that it won't be too tall to fit under bridges and overpasses.

MORE THAN ONE

To carry a lot of cargo, a truck may pull more than one trailer, as with a road-train. By hooking up more than one trailer, they can make the truck very long (left).

◎ CAR TRANSPORTER

Some trailers are made to carry cars. These trailers have two or even three decks. This truck (right) can carry eleven cars at one time!

DUMP TRUCK

Huge dump trucks are needed to carry rocks away from construction sites. Excavators empty the rocks into a container at the back of the dump truck. This container is called the "hopper." The truck then drives to where the load is to be dumped. When it reaches the site, two pistons push the front of the hopper up. The rocks then simply slide out of the back of the hopper.

Counterweight
This dump truck needs a heavy weight to prevent it from tipping over when the hopper dumps out its heavy load.

Hopper
When a truck this size is tipping out its load, the top of the hopper can reach as high as a five-story building!

Wheels
This dump truck has huge wheels—each taller than two adults standing on top of each other!

Pistons
Two pistons raise the front of the dump truck's hopper.

Axle
The axle is where the spinning wheel connects to the truck body.

Drive shaft
The drive shaft delivers power from the engine to the rear wheels.

Canopy
The canopy prevents rubble from falling over the front of the truck.

Cabin
This cab is up so high that the driver has to climb up a ladder to get inside.

Exhaust pipe

ON LOCATION
Some dump trucks are used to transport rocks from mines and quarries that have been dug up by excavators.

Radiator
The radiator is found at the front of the engine. Its job is to prevent the engine from overheating.

Fan
The fan circulates cool air to the engine to also prevent overheating.

Tire
Tracked tires help the truck grip on soft ground.

Engine and fuel tank
The engine that drives a dump truck needs to be very powerful. Its fuel tank holds enough fuel to fill 50 bathtubs!

WORKING ON CONSTRUCTION SITES

Many different trucks work together on construction sites, from diggers and scrapers to concrete mixers and cargo haulers.

Concrete is carried to a construction site in a concrete mixer (below). This has a mixing drum on the back that turns slowly to mix the concrete. When it reaches the site, concrete is poured out through the delivery chute.

Drum fin

The fin is a spiral inside the drum that guides the concrete out of the truck.

Mixing drum

The drum has to turn constantly to mix the water with the concrete.

Delivery chute

This tube can be extended to reach the spot where the concrete is to be poured.

Control panel

The driver can control the delivery chute with these levers.

Water tank

Water is important because it keeps the concrete from hardening in the truck.

PUMPER TRUCK

Sometimes concrete has to be pumped up to high places from a concrete mixer. When this happens, a special pumper truck (left) is used.

LOADER

Loaders (above) are fitted with a huge shovel on the front. They are used to scoop up piles of rocks and earth and dump them in the back of other trucks.

TIPPER TRUCK

A tipper truck (below) carries loads or containers. When the truck reaches the site where the cargo is needed, the rear tilts up and the cargo slides off.

SCRAPER

These large trucks (below) are used to move huge amounts of earth. Underneath the truck is a large blade that skims the ground, digging up the top layer of the soil.

TRUCK DRIVERS

Driving a truck is a tough job. Truck drivers spend many hours on the road all around the world. Since truck drivers spend so much time in their trucks, some trucks are built with many of the comforts of home.

INSTRUMENT PANEL

The instrument panels on the dashboard (left) give the driver information about the truck. The panel includes dials showing speed, distance traveled, engine temperature, and fuel level.

Curtains

Curtains give the driver privacy while sleeping and can also block out the light for daytime nap breaks.

Double bed

If their truck has a bed, drivers can sleep in the truck if there is not a hotel nearby.

SMOOTH FORM

The shape of a tractor is built to be smooth (right). This helps it slip through the air as easily as possible. As a result, the truck uses less fuel, and can carry loads farther.

LIVING AREA

When trucks have living quarters for the driver to use, there may be a bed (left) and washing facilities, including a shower. Some trucks have a small kitchen with a refrigerator, and a place to relax, perhaps with a chair or a desk for doing paperwork.

SUSPENSION

A truck's wheels are fitted with springs and pistons (right). These make the ride smoother for the driver.

Top bunk

When a truck has more than one driver, it is nice to have a second bed.

Closet

Sometimes there is a little closet to hang a change of clothes for the next day.

CRANE TRUCK

Some trucks have a long arm called a "boom" that holds a crane, or hook, that is used for lifting materials high in the air. Once the crane truck arrives at the site, the driver puts down the stabilizers before climbing into the crane cab. Once in the cab, the driver can operate the crane. A telescopic arm moves the crane in and out. A piston moves the arm up and down. The truck crane has two diesel engines—one is used to power the truck, while the other powers the crane.

Turntable

The base of the crane is attached to a turntable. This can turn the crane around in a complete circle.

Crane cab

The driver operates the crane from here. There are levers to turn the crane around and move the end up and down.

Piston

Pistons raise the front of the dump truck's hopper.

Stabilizer

There are four stabilizers, which prevent the truck from falling over when it lifts heavy objects.

Wheels

There are four sets of twin wheels in the back to carry the heavy load. There are also two wheels to steer the front.

Engine

EXTRA HEIGHT

This massive crane truck (left) has a folding boom or "knuckleboom." Some crane trucks can reach up to 47 stories high.

Boom
The arm of the crane can stretch. When it is fully extended, it can reach out over a third of a soccer field.

Boom extension
Sometimes a boom needs to reach high or far away places. An extension lets the boom reach these spots.

Lifting block
Heavy loads are attached to a hook on the end of the lifting block. They are then lifted to where they need to go.

Boom tip
This is where the coil for the crane attaches to the boom.

Leaf-spring
The leaf-spring is one of the oldest types of spring and helps the suspension provide an easier ride.

Hook
The truck can pick up all sorts of materials with this strong hook.

PICKING UP LOADS

Trucks can pick up big and small loads. Some use forks to lift from underneath the load, while others lift from above with a large crane.

FORKLIFT

A forklift truck has two forks at the front. These forks are placed under a load to lift it. The strongest forklift trucks can lift up to 4,000 pounds (1,814 kilograms)! Other lifting trucks may have cranes instead, which lift the cargo high in the air with a thick wire.

Mast
The mast lowers and raises the forks.

Drive wheels
Drive wheels have the power to push the truck.

Engine

Rear wheel
The rear wheel steers the truck in the direction it should go.

Lifting forks
These are used to slide under the load and pick it up.

Counterweight
A forklift must be heavy in the back to prevent it from tipping forward when picking up a large load.

Steering knuckle
This is where the rear wheels are attached and what allows them to steer.

Overhead guard
This protects the driver from heavy, falling objects.

HEAVY-LIFT CRANE

When very large loads need lifting, a heavy-lift crane (right) is used. These huge trucks can have 10 sets of wheels. The arm of the crane can stretch almost the length of a soccer field. As with a smaller truck crane (see pages 18-19), this crane uses stabilizers to keep it steady.

CHERRY PICKER

A cherry picker truck (left) has a platform at the end of an arm. This arm stretches up to reach high above the ground. The whole truck is kept steady by four stabilizers (see page 19).

KNUCKLEBOOM

This huge crane has a boom that folds in the middle, allowing it to lie flat on the truck.

SWIMMING TRUCK

Some special trucks are able to swim across lakes and rivers. They are called "swimming trucks" or "amphibious trucks." When they travel over the ground, they are driven by their wheels, just like normal trucks. However, when they enter the water, propellers spin to push the truck along.

MAKING A BRIDGE

This German amphibious truck (below) is used by the military to carry other vehicles, such as tanks, across a river. It can also be used to make a bridge across a river. Several of these trucks swim alongside each other to help form the bridge. They can make a bridge as long as a soccer field in only 20 minutes!

Pontoon

A pontoon is a flotation device that is able to support itself as well as a heavy load. When lowered, these allow the truck to float in water. They can fold up on top of the truck when it needs to drive on land.

Engine
The engine is at the rear of the vehicle. It drives the vehicle over land and turns the propeller when it is "swimming."

Crane
There is a small crane mounted on the vehicle, used to lift the heavy parts of the bridge into place.

Cab
When the truck drives over ground, the driver sits inside the cab. However, the cab is underwater when the truck is swimming. The driver then uses a set of controls on the roof at the back of the truck.

Ramp
The ramps are laid across the truck when it is being used as a bridge. They also carry the load when the truck is being used as a ferry.

Wheel
This truck has wheels with deep grooves to keep it from slipping on sandy or muddy shores.

NOT JUST ON ROADS

Different trucks are needed for tasks in different environments. Driving over sand is not the same as driving in the snow. These special trucks have unique characteristics suited for where they work.

UNFORTUNATE BEGINNINGS

The first truck was built in 1769 by the Frenchman Nicolas-Joseph Cugnot. It was powered by steam and was built to pull cannons into battle. However, it lost control during testing and was never used again.

ARMORED VEHICLES

Armored trucks are used to carry equipment and soldiers around a battlefield. This armored car (right) weighed as much as five elephants! It was equipped with a gun and had armor to protect the soldiers inside.

Gun
Having a gun on the outside allows soldiers to shoot while staying inside the protection of the truck.

Armored body
The body of a tank is made to withstand heavy gunfire in the midst of a battle.

TRUCKS ON TRACKS

This truck (left) is used to carry out repairs on railroads. It is fitted with special wheels, called "bogies" that allow the truck to drive along the rail tracks.

DESERT TRUCKS

Some trucks have to drive across desert terrain (right). To cope with the rough ground, they need tough suspension (see page 17) and large tires.

ICY TRUCKS

Trucks that drive over ice and snow use extra-wide wheels that are fitted with special snow tires (below). These tires give the truck extra grip and prevent it from sliding around. They also stop the truck from sinking into the snow.

RACING TRUCK

Racing trucks are tractors that are altered to make them go faster. These trucks race each other around race tracks. They are equipped with more powerful engines, allowing them to go much faster than normal trucks. Lightweight materials are used to make the truck as light as possible. Even the glass of the windows and windshield is replaced. These new materials also have to be strong to protect the driver if there is a crash.

Cab
The cabs are equipped with special safety cages to protect the drivers. They also have safety harnesses to prevent the drivers from being thrown around.

Engine
Racing trucks are equipped with very powerful engines. These can be twice as powerful as a normal tractor engine!

GOING FAST

The fastest truck in the world is powered by three jet-fighter engines and can drive at 256 miles (412 kilometers) per hour!

RISKY BUSINESS

While banned in America, this sport is largely popular in Europe. The FIA European Truck Racing Championship features drivers from all over Europe who compete for the title.

Body work

Some racing trucks are fitted with extra sleek parts. These help the trucks drive faster by letting them move through the air as easily as possible.

Brakes

Racing trucks have brakes that get very hot during racing. They are cooled with water to prevent them from getting too hot.

OTHER JOBS TRUCKS DO

Trucks can do all sorts of incredible things. Some trucks are used to transport smaller trucks long distances, while others may haul materials on construction sites. Some trucks are even made for sporting! They may be made to drive fast or large enough to crush smaller cars. All of these jobs require trucks to be very strong.

TOW TRUCK

Sometimes a car or truck breaks down and cannot drive any farther. When this happens, a tow truck (below) will attach a hook to the vehicle and lift one end. The tow truck then pulls the broken vehicle to a garage where it can be fixed.

Towing crane
The tow truck uses this crane to hook onto cars that need to be towed away.

Exhaust pipe

Fuel tank

Engine

RACING TEAM TRUCK

These trucks (right) carry the cars and equipment for a motor racing team. At the end of the race, the trucks are loaded up and driven off to the next event.

FUN TRUCKS

Many trucks are altered to be able to do special things. Some of them can do wheelies (left) while others are made to jump from one ramp to another over a long row of cars. There are even freestyle truck competitions where drivers are judged on different types of cool stunts they can perform with their truck.

MONSTER TRUCK

Big trucks called "monster trucks" have huge wheels and crush other cars when they drive over them (right).

GLOSSARY

Amphibious truck
A road truck that can also swim. Its engine drives both the wheels and a propeller.

Armored vehicles
These machines are designed to withstand harsh conditions such as ice, extreme heat, or even a battle.

Bogies
These are special wheels that are built to run on rail tracks.

Boom
The arm of a crane.

Cab
The part of the truck where the driver sits.

Cherry picker
A truck that has a platform on the end of an arm. This arm can extend, lifting the platform to high places.

Concrete mixer
Concrete must be transported by special trucks with a mixing drum and water tank to keep the concrete from hardening inside the truck.

Diesel
A type of fuel that is used in truck engines.

Drum brake
A special brake designed for large trucks. It is created to withstand the large force created by a heavy load moving at high speeds.

Dump truck
These have a deep bed for carrying dirt and rubble on construction sites. The bed can tip to the back or side to dump out the load.

Engine
Converts fuel into energy to power the truck.

Exhaust
The pipe where fumes created by the engine can exit the truck.

Fifth wheel skid plate
This rotating plate is where the trailer attaches to the tractor and helps improve the truck's ability to turn.

Forklift
These trucks have two forks that lift a big or small load and carry it a short distance.

Lowboy
A truck with an open trailer that is made to carry very large, heavy loads, such as other trucks.

Monster truck
Trucks that are made with huge wheels that can crush other cars when driving over them.

Pickup
A smaller truck that can carry a small load in the flat bed in the back.

Racing trucks
These trucks are altered to make them go as fast as possible for competitions.

Radiator
Located at the front of the truck, it circulates coolant to cool down the engine and prevent overheating.

Shock absorber
These attach the wheels to the body of the truck and reduce the amount of force put on the truck from a bumpy road.

Stabilizer
These sit on the ground and keep the truck from tipping over when lifting a heavy load.

Suspension
A system of springs and other devices that smooth the ride of a truck.

Tanker
Trucks designed to carry large loads of liquid, like gasoline or milk.

Tractor
The front part of a tractor-trailer. The driver sits in the tractor to drive the truck. It also contains the engine.

Tractor-trailer truck
A truck that comes in two or more parts. At the front is the tractor that pulls one or more trailers.

Trailer
Towed behind a truck or tractor, the trailer is the part that carries the load or cargo.

Turntable
The rotating table that attaches a crane to a truck and spins in all directions.

INDEX

PHOTO CREDITS
Abbreviations: t-top, m-middle, b-bottom, r-right, l-left, c-center. Pages 4, 15lb – Roger Vlitos. 7lb – Foden/Paccar. 10b, 11m, 15lt, 16, 17b & m – Peterbilt/Paccar. 9, 15br, 19 – Spectrum Colour Library. 11b, 25m, 27t, 29m – Eye Ubiquitous. 21 all, 25t – Liebherr. 22 – EWK. 25b – James Davis Travel Photography. 29t – Renault. 29b – Frank Spooner Pictures. 27 m – By Go4more at en.wikipedia (Public domain), from Wikimedia Commons. 24 – By MdeVicente (Own work) (CC0), via Wikimedia Commons